··· A **TIMELINE HISTORY** OF THE ···

EARLY AMERICAN REPUBLIC

TIMELINE TRACKERS : AMERICA'S BEGINNINGS ···

ALLAN MOREY

Lerner Publications Company
Minneapolis

CONTENTS

Lerner Publications Company
A division of Lerner Publishing Group, Inc.
241 First Avenue North
Minneapolis, MN 55401 USA

For reading levels and more information, look up
this title at www.lernerbooks.com.

Library of Congress Cataloging-in-Publication Data

Morey, Allan.
    A timeline history of the early American republic
/ by Allan Morey.
        pages   cm. — (Timeline trackers: America's
beginnings)
    Includes index.
    ISBN 978–1–4677–3641–1 (lib. bdg. : alk. paper)
    ISBN 978–1–4677–4753–0 (eBook)
    1. United States—History—1783–1865—
Chronology—Juvenile literature. 2. United States—
History—Revolution, 1775–1783—Chronology—
Juvenile literature. I. Title.
E301.M59 2015
973.2—dc23   2013041489

Manufactured in the United States of America
1 – BP – 7/15/14

COVER PHOTO:
American general George Washington and French general Jean-Baptiste Donatien de Vimeur, comte de Rochambeau, give final orders before attack during the Battle of Yorktown.

INTRODUCTION

During the Revolutionary War (1775–1783), a ragtag band of colonists pitted themselves against the deadly British redcoats—and won! Once the smoke cleared, however, their struggles were not over. The American colonists had earned the right to govern themselves. Yet they did not agree on how their new government should be formed.

The former colonies had become individual states in a new nation. A document called the Articles of Confederation united the states under a central government. The Articles established the United States as a republic. But they did not create a strong central government to manage that republic.

The years following the war were difficult ones. The country could not raise money to pay its war debts. And tensions grew among the states. The country's leaders knew the Articles of Confederation needed to be changed. Otherwise, their new nation might fall apart. So they set to work on a new document.

This document would become known as the US Constitution. With it, the Founding Fathers established important guiding principles. These ideas laid out how to create and run a successful government. They helped bind the struggling country into a strong, democratic nation.

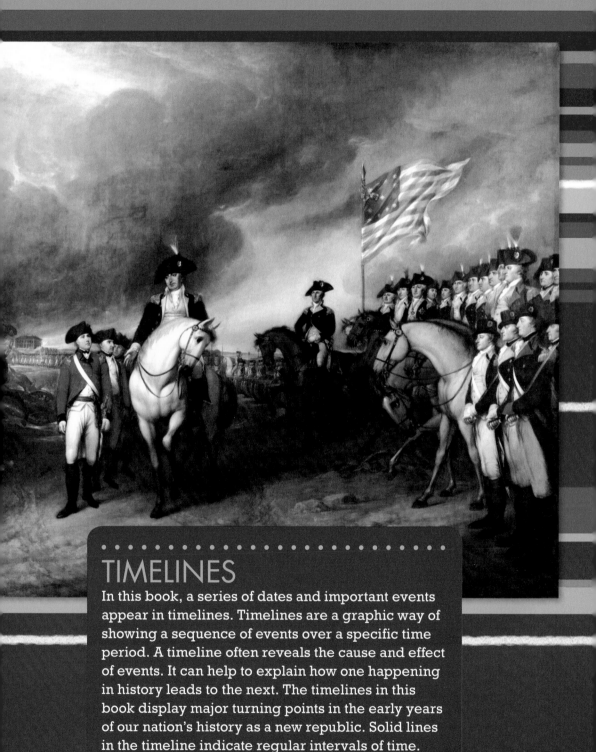

TIMELINES

In this book, a series of dates and important events appear in timelines. Timelines are a graphic way of showing a sequence of events over a specific time period. A timeline often reveals the cause and effect of events. It can help to explain how one happening in history leads to the next. The timelines in this book display major turning points in the early years of our nation's history as a new republic. Solid lines in the timeline indicate regular intervals of time. Dashed lines represent bigger jumps in time.

CHAPTER 1

BIRTH of a NATION

Before forming a single nation, the US colonies often acted independently. They set up their own armies and legislatures. But when war broke out, colonial leaders felt the colonies needed to act as one.

Articles of Confederation

Together, American leaders created the Articles of Confederation. This document established the new nation's central government. The Articles of Confederation officially went into effect on March 1, 1781.

Many Americans feared an overly powerful central government. They did not want to live under the kind of rule they'd experienced as colonists. So the Articles purposely created a weak central government. That left a lot of power in the hands of the states.

The government had the power to handle relationships with foreign governments. It also organized the war effort against

June 15, 1775: George Washington becomes commander and chief of the Continental Army.

1775   1776   1777

Apr. 19, 1775: The Revolutionary War begins.

July 4, 1776: The Declaration of Independence comes into effect.

Great Britain. But the central government had no power to collect taxes. It couldn't pass laws, either. It didn't even have a single leader to oversee the government and the states.

Instead, a Confederation Congress ran the central government. The Congress contained between two and seven delegates from each state. But each state had only one vote in the Congress.

The Articles of Confederation helped establish the central government's role within the new nation.

Nov. 15, 1777: The Continental Congress approves the Articles.

1778   1779   1780   1781

1778–1781: The states debate and eventually ratify the Articles.

Mar. 1, 1781: The Articles of Confederation are ratified.

Treaty of Paris

A major battle in the Revolutionary War took place in 1781. General George Washington led the Continental Army to victory in Yorktown, Virginia. This Battle of Yorktown forced the British to surrender.

Next came peace talks between the United States and Great Britain. Three Americans represented the United States in these talks. They were John Adams, Benjamin Franklin, and John Jay. Each man had played an important role in the struggle for independence. Adams had helped inspire the

George Washington and others in the Continental Army arrive in New York after their victory.

Sept. 28, 1781: The Battle of Yorktown begins.

1780

1781

1782

Mar. 1, 1781: The Confederation Congress holds its first session, which lasts until November 3.

Oct. 19, 1781: British general Charles Cornwallis surrenders at Yorktown.

colonies to fight for their freedom. He also helped shape the ideas in the Declaration of Independence. Franklin had helped gain France's support during the war. And Jay had persuaded Spain to lend the United States money.

These three Americans convinced Great Britain to recognize the United States as an independent nation. The British also agreed to give the United States more land. The new land extended west to the Mississippi River. Having control of these lands would allow the new nation to grow.

This agreement became known as the Treaty of Paris. When it was signed in 1783, it officially ended the Revolutionary War. It also established the United States as an equal nation among powerful European countries.

AMERICAN INDIANS IN THE EARLY REPUBLIC

During the Revolutionary War, most American Indian tribes sided with Great Britain. The British had promised to protect American Indian lands from the Americans. But after the war, Great Britain gave the United States control over those lands.

At the time, many Americans did not respect or understand American Indians. American Indians were given very few rights in the new nation. And settlers eventually moved onto their lands. That caused many future conflicts.

Sept. 27, 1782: Peace talks begin with Great Britain.

Sept. 3, 1783: The Treaty of Paris is signed.

Jan. 14, 1784: Congress ratifies the Treaty of Paris.

1783

1784

1785

Dec. 1783: George Washington retires from the military and politics to lead a quiet life.

Mar. 1, 1784: Virginian Thomas Jefferson proposes a way to establish new states on western US lands.

CHAPTER 2

HARD TIMES

After the war, the people of the United States looked forward to good years ahead. But freedom did not mean their troubles were over. The cost of the war weighed heavily on the new nation. The United States had borrowed millions of dollars from European countries. This debt equaled more than $250 billion in modern money. That money needed to be paid back. The new government also owed pay to thousands of American soldiers who had fought in the war.

Money Troubles

Normally, a government raised money by requiring citizens to pay taxes. But the Articles of Confederation did not give the central government that power. At the beginning of the war, the states had

American soldiers were directly affected by the financial debt the United States had acquired.

1784–1785: The United States suffers through difficult economic times.

FEB. 1784   MARCH 1784   APRIL 1784   MAY 1784

Feb. 22, 1784: The United States sends its first trade ship to China.

Apr. 23, 1784: The central government calls for newly claimed western lands to be divided into separate states.

MONEY TROUBLES

promised to provide funds. They were having money troubles of their own, though. So they were slow to send money to the central government.

Businessman Robert Morris from Pennsylvania was in charge of managing the government's money. Morris argued that the government should be allowed to collect taxes to pay its debts.

Alexander Hamilton agreed. He was a member of the Confederation Congress from New York. Hamilton and Morris proposed an amendment to the Articles of Confederation. The amendment would give the central government the power to tax citizens directly. But Congress quickly voted against this idea.

This statue of Robert Morris stands in front of Independence Hall in Philadelphia, Pennsylvania.

July 4, 1784: Some states celebrate their first Fourth of July as part of a new nation.

Sept. 21, 1784: The *Pennsylvania Packet and Daily Advertiser* becomes the nation's first daily newspaper.

JULY 1784   AUG. 1784   SEPT. 1784   OCT. 1784

Aug. 23, 1784: People in the western part of North Carolina declare independence from the rest of the state. They try to form their own state, called Franklin.

Oct. 22, 1784: The Treaty of Fort Stanwix is signed between the United States and a group of American Indian tribes called the Six Nations of the Iroquois.

Tensions among the States

The British were not happy about losing so much land to the United States. So Great Britain did not make things easy for the new nation. It had once been a major buyer of American goods. After the war, it decided to close its markets to American trade. Suddenly, Americans could no longer sell enough of their crops and goods.

George Washington's home, called Mount Vernon, was a frequent meeting spot for representatives from the states.

Dec. 21, 1784:
John Jay becomes the first secretary of state.

DEC. 1784　　　JAN. 1785　　　FEB. 1785

Jan. 21, 1785:
The United States enters into a treaty with the Wyandot American Indian tribe and several other tribes.

Growing tensions among the states were also hurting the country. The Articles did not give the central government the ability to control trade between states. That power was left to each individual state. But states did not always deal fairly with one another. A state might charge higher taxes on goods from one of its neighbors than from another. This weakened trust among the states.

The taxes on goods also harmed individual Americans. These taxes caused the price of goods to go up. Fewer people could afford to buy them. And traders and farmers suffered. Unemployment rose, and many Americans went into debt.

Meanwhile, the states were also in debt after the war. The taxes they charged helped with those debts. But the taxes also angered many Americans.

Many farmers struggled during the republic's early years.

May 20, 1785: Congress begins selling land west of the original thirteen colonies to raise money.

Mar. 1785   **Apr. 1785**   **May 1785**   **June 1785**

Mar. 28, 1785: Maryland and Virginia sign the Mount Vernon Compact. It gives both states free access to the Potomac River.

May 16, 1785: The Confederation Congress denies western North Carolina the right to become an independent state.

Shays's Rebellion

Farmers in western Massachusetts were among the Americans who struggled the most. They had borrowed money to start up new farms. But they could not sell their crops. That meant they had no money to pay the debts they owed. On top of that, the Massachusetts state government demanded that its citizens pay more taxes. The farmers could not pay these taxes either. Hundreds of farmers lost their land or were sent to jail because of their debts. This further angered local citizens.

Daniel Shays and Luke Day both had been captains in the Continental Army. On August 29, 1786, they led a group of protesters to the town of Northampton. There they shut down the court that was ruling against farmers in debt. That fall

This artwork shows Daniel Shays *(left)* standing next to a British colonial.

Jan. 3, 1786: The Choctaw American Indians sign on to the Treaty of Hopewell with the United States.

Jan. 10, 1786: The Chickasaw American Indians sign on to the Treaty of Hopewell.

Nov. 1785   **Dec. 1785**   **Jan. 1786**   **Feb. 1786**

Nov. 28, 1785: The first Treaty of Hopewell is signed between the US government and members of the Cherokee tribe.

Jan. 30, 1786: The United States signs a peace treaty with the Shawnee American Indians of Ohio.

they continued to shut down court after court in the western part of the state.

In January 1787, Shays and his followers tried to take control of government weapons stored in Springfield, Massachusetts. The central government did not have the power or the money to send an army. So that meant the government could not defend its weapons. Instead, state soldiers defeated Shays's forces. Their protests eventually died down by the summer of 1787. But people feared other rebellions might start up in other states.

The Massachusetts military, illustrated here, defeats the rioters of Shays's Rebellion in 1787.

Aug. 29, 1786: Daniel Shays and Luke Day lead a mob of rioters to shut down the courthouse at Northampton.

Aug. 1786   **Sept. 1786**   **Jan. 1787**   **Feb. 1787**

Aug. 22, 1786: At a meeting in Hatfield, Massachusetts, citizens express their unhappiness with the state government and its new taxes.

Sept. 5, 1786: Protesters shut down the court in Worcester, Massachusetts.

Jan. 25, 1787: Shays leads a force to capture federal weapons in Springfield.

Annapolis Convention

Shays's Rebellion struck fear in many Americans. They argued that the government needed the money and power to create its own army. That way, it could protect citizens from violent protests.

Others argued for fairer trade agreements among the states. One such agreement was known as the Mount Vernon Compact. In 1785 it had helped to establish peace and trust between Maryland and Virginia. The people who created the compact felt the country would be better off if all states operated under the same trade laws. But the central government had no power to establish such laws.

These two problems highlighted some of the weaknesses in the Articles of Confederation. Many state leaders

This artwork from the 1800s shows the Maryland State House in Annapolis, Maryland.

Nov. 1786: States begin electing delegates to the Constitutional Convention.

Sept. 14, 1786: The Annapolis Convention ends.

SEPT. 1786   OCT. 1786   NOV. 1786   DEC. 1786

Sept. 11, 1786: The Annapolis Convention begins.

Oct. 11, 1786: A government committee is created to review a report of the Annapolis Convention.

felt that the Articles needed to be changed. Some of these leaders held a meeting in Annapolis, Maryland, to discuss changes. But only delegates from New Jersey, New York, Pennsylvania, Delaware, and Virginia attended the Annapolis Convention. Some delegates from other states did not arrive in time. Others did not support the changes being discussed. They worried about giving the central government too much power.

The delegates in Annapolis called for a Constitutional Convention. This meeting would include all the states. There, delegates could address growing concerns and work toward creating a better government.

TREATY OF HOPEWELL

Tensions between the US government and American Indians grew during the 1780s. Conflicts often arose over valuable farmland in the South. In 1785 the US government signed the Treaty of Hopewell with the Cherokee tribe. The treaty set aside an area of land for the Cherokee people. Settlers would not be allowed onto it. The US government hoped that the treaty would encourage peace between European Americans and the Cherokee. The United States went on to sign similar agreements with other American Indian communities.

Feb. 28, 1787: The Confederation Congress endorses a meeting for a Constitutional Convention.

May 25, 1787: The Constitutional Convention begins.

JAN. 1787   FEB. 1787   MAY 1787   JUNE 1787

May 14, 1787: The first delegates from Virginia and Pennsylvania arrive for the Constitutional Convention.

Summer 1787: George Washington reluctantly agrees to serve as president of the convention.

CHAPTER 3

DRAFTING the US CONSTITUTION

The Constitutional Convention took place in Philadelphia, Pennsylvania. Each state sent between two and eight delegates to the meeting. Only Rhode Island did not attend the convention. This small state worried that changes to the Articles of Confederation would favor larger states.

At first, the fifty-five delegates planned only to revise the Articles. But they soon realized that the document had too many problems. Bigger changes were needed. The United States would still be a republic. But it needed a more powerful central, or federal, government.

To lay the groundwork for these changes, the country needed a blueprint. A new document must replace the Articles of Confederation. This document would become known as the United States Constitution.

The Virginia Plan

Edmund Randolph was a delegate from Virginia, the most

THE VIRGINIA PLAN

May 29, 1787: Edmund Randolph proposes the Virginia Plan.

May 30, 1787: Delegates agree that a national government should consist of the three branches from the Virginia Plan.

MAY 28   MAY 29   MAY 30   MAY 31

May 28–29, 1787: Rules of conducting business are established for the Constitutional Convention.

May 31, 1787: Delegates reject the idea that the second house of Congress should be voted into office by the first house.

populous state. He presented the first plan for a new government. It had been written by another Virginia leader, James Madison. Madison's Virginia Plan called for three branches of government. The legislative branch would create laws. The executive branch would enforce them. And the judiciary branch would provide a national court system.

Madison's plan also called for the legislature to be divided into two sections, a house and a senate. And it argued that states with greater populations should have more lawmakers in the legislature. That would give the larger states—especially Virginia—more power in the government than smaller ones.

In addition, the Virginia Plan gave the central government the power to regulate trade among states. It also gave the government the power to enforce laws with its own army.

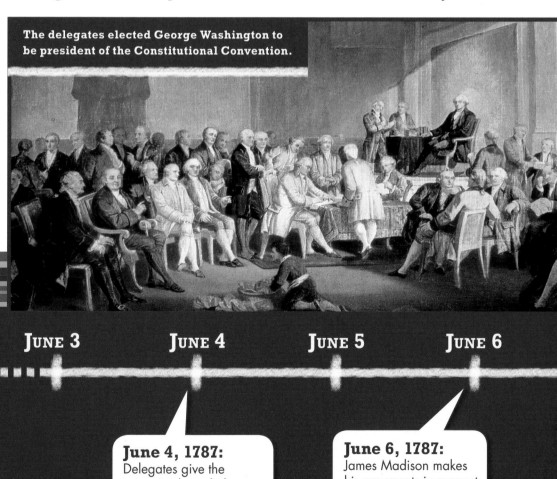

The delegates elected George Washington to be president of the Constitutional Convention.

JUNE 3   JUNE 4   JUNE 5   JUNE 6

June 4, 1787:
Delegates give the executive branch the power to reject laws from Congress with a veto.

June 6, 1787:
James Madison makes his arguments in support of the Virginia Plan.

New Jersey Plan

Delegates from small states liked the idea of three branches of government. But they disagreed that states with greater populations should have more lawmakers in Congress. That part of the Virginia Plan seemed unfair to them.

Roger Sherman and Oliver Ellsworth were both delegates from Connecticut. They proposed a compromise. They suggested that the House of Representatives would be based on a state's population. But each state would have only one lawmaker in the Senate. Large states felt this idea favored small states too much. They rejected the plan.

William Paterson

William Paterson was from the small state of New Jersey. He presented another idea. His New Jersey Plan proposed that all states have an equal number of lawmakers in Congress. He also suggested that there be only one house in the legislature. This plan was also voted down. But it helped keep the debate alive.

The delegates did not dismiss every idea in the New Jersey Plan, however.

June 9, 1787: Delegates vote against having state governors elect the president.

June 14, 1787: New Jersey delegates ask for voting to be delayed on the Virginia Plan.

JUNE 9 JUNE 10 JUNE 11 JUNE 14

June 1787: Shays's Rebellion ends.

June 11, 1787: Roger Sherman and Oliver Ellsworth propose their two-house idea for Congress.

Paterson suggested that the executive branch select justices to the Supreme Court. His plan also gave the national government the power to tax citizens directly. Another important idea was that national laws would outweigh state laws. All of these ideas would eventually make it into the US Constitution.

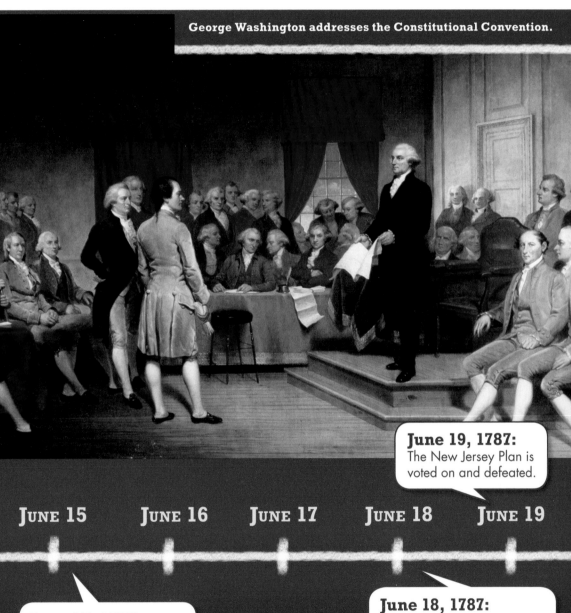

George Washington addresses the Constitutional Convention.

June 19, 1787:
The New Jersey Plan is voted on and defeated.

JUNE 15   JUNE 16   JUNE 17   JUNE 18   JUNE 19

June 15, 1787:
William Paterson introduces the New Jersey Plan.

June 18, 1787:
Alexander Hamilton proposes his own plan, which supports a strong central government and a president for life.

The Connecticut Compromise

Support for a two-house legislature remained strong among the delegates. But heated debates continued over the number of lawmakers each state would have. Toward the end of June, Oliver Ellsworth and Roger Sherman proposed a new plan. It is often called the Connecticut Compromise, or the Great Compromise.

Ellsworth and Sherman argued that each state should

Oliver Ellsworth

have an equal number of lawmakers in the Senate. The House of Representatives would be based on state population. Each state would get one representative for every forty thousand inhabitants. This idea was similar to a proposal they had made weeks earlier. But there were a couple of key differences.

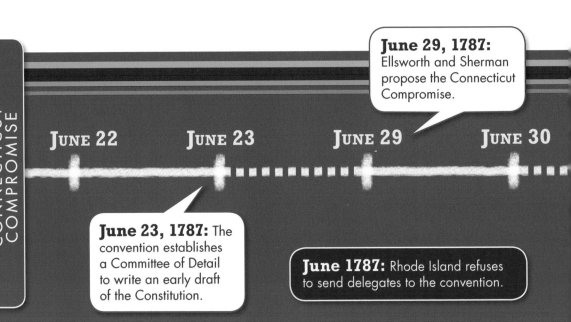

CONNECTICUT COMPROMISE

June 29, 1787: Ellsworth and Sherman propose the Connecticut Compromise.

JUNE 22   **JUNE 23**   **JUNE 29**   **JUNE 30**

June 23, 1787: The convention establishes a Committee of Detail to write an early draft of the Constitution.

June 1787: Rhode Island refuses to send delegates to the convention.

Each state would have two seats in the Senate instead of one. That change pleased the smaller states because they would have more lawmakers. The plan also gave the House of Representatives the power to propose how the government would raise and spend money. The Senate would be able to vote on these bills, but not change them. This pleased the larger states. It gave them more say in deciding how the government used its money.

This artist rendition shows Roger Sherman and Oliver Ellsworth drafting the Great Compromise.

In the end, the Great Compromise used ideas from both the Virginia and the New Jersey Plans. This mixing of ideas earned the delegates' approval.

July 12, 1787: Delegates agree that a national census will be held every ten years. The census will count how many people live in each state.

JULY 11   JULY 12   JULY 13   JULY 14

July 13, 1787: The Northwest Ordinance of 1787 establishes the Northwest Territory. This area includes the land south of the Great Lakes and northwest of the Ohio River.

Electoral College

The Great Compromise settled some important disagreements at the Constitutional Convention. Yet debate continued over how to select the nation's leader. The Virginia and New Jersey Plans gave that power to the lawmakers in Congress.

Some delegates worried that such a policy would cause corruption in Congress. Lawmakers might bargain for votes to become president. They might promise favors to one another. Or they might offer one another money in order to gain power.

James Wilson

These activities would not be democratic.

The delegates also tossed out the idea of a direct vote by American citizens. They worried that the general public was not well informed. People might only vote for candidates from their own state. Then larger states would have more power in presidential elections.

Some delegates at the Constitutional Convention proposed another compromise. They suggested a system known

July 17, 1787: Delegates unanimously agree that there should be a single executive, or president.

Aug. 8, 1787: Delegates agree that each state should have at least one member in the House of Representatives.

JULY 17 JULY 18 JULY 19 AUG. 8

July 19, 1787: Delegates agree that electors will be selected by each state's legislature to vote for the president.

as the Electoral College. It would be an indirect way to elect a president. Each state would select men called electors to vote for the president. The number of electors for a state would equal its combined number of senators and representatives. After some debate, the delegates approved this plan.

SLAVES AND THE CONSTITUTION

Some delegates in northern states called for an end to slavery. But many states relied on the labor of enslaved African Americans. These states refused to give up their unpaid workers.

Slaves had no rights as US citizens. They could not vote or own property. Yet slaveholding states wanted to count slaves as part of their populations.

This plan would give slave states more power in Congress. Many states without slaves disliked this idea. The delegates finally decided that every five slaves would equal three people in population counts.

Aug. 15, 1787: Delegates agree that a three-fourths vote from each house of Congress can override a presidential veto.

Sept. 4, 1787: Delegates approve the proposal for an Electoral College.

AUG. 15   AUG. 22   SEPT. 4   SEPT. 5   SEPT. 6

Aug. 22, 1787: Charles Pinckney from South Carolina warns that southern states will not sign a constitution that opposes slavery.

Sept. 6, 1787: Delegates agree that the president and the vice president will serve four-year terms.

CHAPTER 4

NEW BEGINNINGS

In September 1787, thirty-nine delegates signed the US Constitution. Several delegates did not attend the signing. They did not approve of everything in the Constitution. But the document had enough signatures to move on to the next step. It was time for the states to ratify the Constitution.

Ratifying the Constitution

Nine of the thirteen states needed to ratify the Constitution before it could become law. Many of the smaller states were quick to sign on. The Constitution offered them protection from powerful larger states. It gave smaller states a more equal role in government. These and other supporters of a strong federal government became known as Federalists.

Leaders from other states were more suspicious of the Constitution. Some of the Constitution's critics were called Anti-Federalists. Anti-Federalists wanted to protect the power of the states. They worried that the US Constitution gave the

RATIFYING THE CONSTITUTION

Sept. 12, 1787: George Mason from Virginia first proposes a Bill of Rights at the Constitutional Convention. The idea is rejected.

Aug. 1787   Sept. 1787   Oct. 1787   Nov. 1787

Sept. 17, 1787: Delegates at the Constitutional Convention vote in favor of the US Constitution.

Sept. 28, 1787: The Confederation Congress calls for states to ratify the US Constitution.

federal government too much control. They also felt that the document did not properly protect the rights of American citizens.

Anti-Federalists in Massachusetts were especially powerful. They questioned whether their state should even ratify the Constitution. Massachusetts was a big and important state. If it rejected the Constitution, other states might too.

That's when Governor John Hancock stepped in. He proposed the Massachusetts Compromise. This plan called for a Bill of Rights. It would be a set of additions, or amendments, to the Constitution. These amendments would protect the rights of individual Americans. The plan allowed his state to ratify the Constitution. At a later date, the states would need to approve the Bill of Rights.

John Hancock

Dec. 12, 1787: Pennsylvania joins the nation.

Dec. 18, 1787: New Jersey joins the nation.

Jan. 9, 1788: Connecticut joins the nation.

Feb. 6, 1788: Massachusetts joins the nation and recommends a Bill of Rights.

DEC. 1787   **JAN. 1788**   **FEB. 1788**   **MARCH 1788**

Dec. 7, 1787: Delaware becomes the first state to officially enter the new nation by ratifying the US Constitution.

Jan. 2, 1788: Georgia joins the nation.

Jan. 30, 1788: The Massachusetts Compromise is proposed.

The Federalist Papers

Getting Massachusetts to ratify the Constitution was a big victory for the Federalists. But some states still hesitated to approve the document. A small group of Federalists set out to convince those remaining states. They published a series of important articles and essays known as the Federalist Papers. Authors of the Federalist Papers included Alexander Hamilton, James Madison, and John Jay.

James Madison

Federalists laid out an argument for a strong federal government. They stated that such a government would bind the individual states into a unified nation. It would also allow the United States to become a more powerful and secure nation.

The Federalist Papers also discussed the system of checks and balances built into the Constitution. These limits on each branch of government would ensure that no single branch ever had too much power. For example,

John Jay

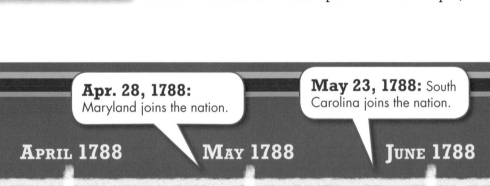

Apr. 28, 1788: Maryland joins the nation.

May 23, 1788: South Carolina joins the nation.

APRIL 1788 **MAY 1788** **JUNE 1788**

Spring 1788: Hamilton, Madison, and Jay publish the Federalist Papers.

the Constitution gave the legislative branch the power to create laws. Yet it also gave the executive branch the power to veto unfair laws. And the judiciary branch could review and overturn unfair laws. Such checks and balances assured that the government remained just.

The Federalist Papers helped convince more states to ratify the Constitution, which became the law of the land in July 1788.

The Federalist Papers were a series of eighty-five essays in support of the Constitution.

Alexander Hamilton

THE

FEDERALIST:

A COLLECTION OF

ESSAYS,

WRITTEN IN FAVOUR OF THE

NEW CONSTITUTION,

AS AGREED-UPON BY THE

FEDERAL CONVENTION,

SEPTEMBER 17, 1787.

IN TWO VOLUMES.
VOL. I.

June 21, 1788:
New Hampshire is the ninth state to join the nation, making the US Constitution official.

July 26, 1788:
New York joins the nation.

JULY 1788   AUG. 1788   SEPT. 1788

June 25, 1788:
Virginia joins the nation.

July 2, 1788:
The Confederation Congress accepts the ratification of the US Constitution.

Aug. 2, 1788:
North Carolina at first votes against ratifying the Constitution.

Washington's Election

With the approval of the Constitution came the first presidential election. It began early in 1789. First, each state selected electors to the Electoral College. In some states, the state legislature selected the electors. In other states, voters chose the electors.

At the time, only white men who owned property could vote. Many Founding Fathers believed only citizens who paid property taxes should have a say in government. Another belief was that only white, male landowners were intelligent enough to vote. Because of this policy, less than 2 percent of Americans were actually able to vote in the first election.

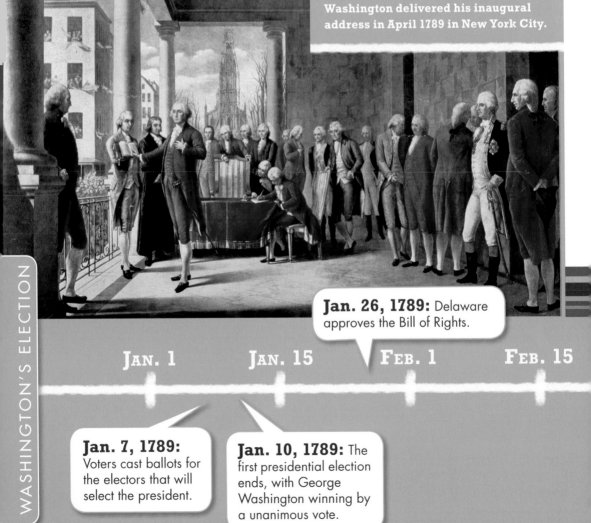

Washington delivered his inaugural address in April 1789 in New York City.

Jan. 26, 1789: Delaware approves the Bill of Rights.

JAN. 1   JAN. 15   FEB. 1   FEB. 15

Jan. 7, 1789: Voters cast ballots for the electors that will select the president.

Jan. 10, 1789: The first presidential election ends, with George Washington winning by a unanimous vote.

Each state's electors were then given the power to vote for a president. The candidate receiving the most votes would become president. One candidate for president was George Washington. He had gained fame as the leader of the Continental Army during the Revolutionary War. He had hoped to retire after the war, but his country needed him. Many Americans respected him as an honest and skillful leader. They trusted him to lead the country.

The electors agreed. They unanimously elected Washington as the first president of the United States. They elected John Adams as vice president.

John Adams

ELECTING A VICE PRESIDENT

The Constitution stated that the president and the vice president were to be elected separately. The candidate with the most votes became president. The candidate with the second most votes became vice president. In 1804 the Twelfth Amendment changed this rule. From then on, the president and the vice president were elected together.

Mar. 4, 1789:
The First US Congress meets.

MAR. 1   MAR. 15   APR. 1   APR. 15

Mar. 10, 1789:
Pennsylvania approves the Bill of Rights.

Mar. 27, 1789:
New York approves the Bill of Rights.

Washington's Cabinet

The US Constitution called for a single president to lead the executive branch. That did not mean the president worked alone. The vice president advised the president on how to run the country. The Constitution also gave the president the ability to choose other advisers, known as the cabinet. These advisers would lead major governmental departments.

Washington's first government cabinet was established in 1789.

Early in Washington's first term, Congress set up three departments. They were the Department of State, the Department of the Treasury, and the Department of War. The leaders of these departments made up the president's cabinet.

Washington chose Thomas Jefferson to lead the State Department. Jefferson

Apr. 30, 1789: George Washington's first term as president begins.

June 11, 1789: Rhode Island approves the Bill of Rights.

APRIL 1789   **MAY 1789**   **JUNE 1789**   **JULY 1789**

June 8, 1789: In Congress, James Madison argues in favor of the Bill of Rights.

June 27, 1789: The Department of War is established.

had penned the Declaration of Independence. He had also served in the Confederation Congress. In his new job, he advised Washington on dealings with foreign countries.

Alexander Hamilton became the first secretary of the treasury. He advised the president on how to handle the government's finances. Washington asked Henry Knox to be secretary of war. Knox had served with Washington during the Revolutionary War. His job was to advise the president on US military matters.

Washington also asked Edmund Randolph from Virginia to become attorney general. Randolph did not have a department to head. But he served as the president's legal adviser. Together, Washington's cabinet helped shape the new nation.

George Washington

Sept. 11, 1789:
Alexander Hamilton becomes the first secretary of the treasury.

Aug. 1789   **Sept. 1789**   **Oct. 1789**   **Nov. 1789**

July 27, 1789:
The Department of State is established.

Sept. 2, 1789:
The Department of the Treasury is established.

Sept. 12, 1789:
Henry Knox becomes the first secretary of war.

The Supreme Court

When Washington became president, the country had no federal courts. So Congress soon passed the Judiciary Act. This law set up the beginnings of a federal court system. That included the creation of the US Supreme Court, the highest court in the land.

The Judiciary Act stated that the Supreme Court would be made up of six judges. The US Constitution said that the president would appoint Supreme Court judges. It also said that the judges were to serve for life. Washington selected John Jay as the chief justice, the head of the Supreme Court. Then he selected the other judges on the court.

The nation's Founding Fathers designed the Supreme Court to be the nation's most powerful court. But it started out as the weakest branch of government. The Constitution did not spell out exactly what powers the Supreme

John Blair, Jr. from Virginia was one of five associate Supreme Court Justices. The others were John Rutledge, William Cushing, James Wilson, and James Iredell.

Sept. 26, 1789: Edmund Randolph becomes the first US attorney general.

Sept. 24, 1789: The Judiciary Act is signed into law.

SEPT. 1   SEPT. 15   OCT. 1   OCT. 15

Sept. 24, 1789: President Washington selects John Jay to be the first Supreme Court chief justice.

Sept. 25, 1789: Congress sends a ten-amendment Bill of Rights to the states to ratify.

Court had. In its early years, the court ruled on few major cases.

The court's role did not begin to change until the nineteenth century. Since then the court has ruled on cases that cannot be properly settled in a state court system. It also rules on laws passed by state and federal lawmakers. The court often determines how a law is to be carried out. And it rules on whether a law is constitutional. The modern Supreme Court has nine judges. After hearing a case, the judges vote on a decision. Once the Supreme Court makes a decision, it is final.

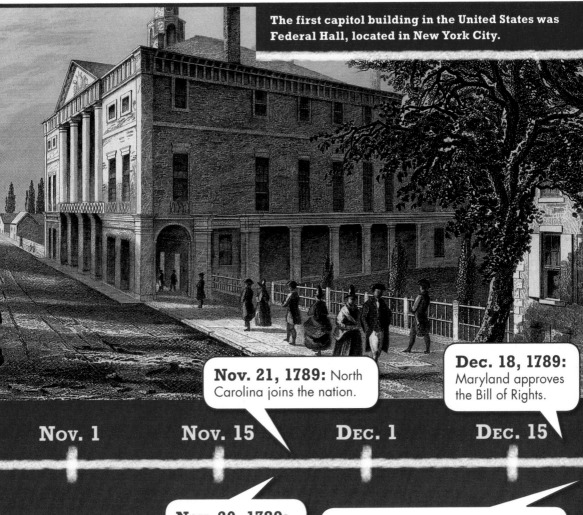

The first capitol building in the United States was Federal Hall, located in New York City.

Nov. 21, 1789: North Carolina joins the nation.

Dec. 18, 1789: Maryland approves the Bill of Rights.

Nov. 1   Nov. 15   Dec. 1   Dec. 15

Nov. 20, 1789: New Jersey approves the Bill of Rights.

Dec. 23, 1789: Maryland and Virginia agree to give up land along the Potomac River for a federal capital city.

CHAPTER 5

MORE WORK TO BE DONE

George Washington started many important traditions during his early years as president. One of the first was a speech he gave to Congress in January 1790. It was originally called the Annual Message. We know it as the State of the Union address.

The First State of the Union

Washington took the idea for his speech from the US Constitution. It says that the president "shall from time to time give to the Congress Information on the State of the Union." This meant that the president would discuss the nation's strengths and weaknesses. He might also talk about challenges the country faced and recommend actions for Congress to consider.

In his speech, Washington said that the country was enjoying a time of peace and prosperity. Yet work still needed to be done. Washington went on to discuss his goals for the

Jan. 8, 1790: George Washington gives the first Annual Message, now known as the State of the Union address.

Jan. 25, 1790: New Hampshire approves the Bill of Rights

JAN. 1790   FEB. 1790   MAR. 1790

Jan. 19, 1790: South Carolina approves the Bill of Rights.

Feb. 1, 1790: The Supreme Court holds its first session.

nation's future. One of these goals was to establish a national army. A strong military would protect the United States from attacks by foreign countries and American Indians.

Washington talked too about the need for a national currency. At the time, each state made its own money. Washington believed all Americans should use the same money. He also talked about foreigners coming to live in the United States from other countries. He said the nation needed to determine how a foreign person could become a US citizen. Washington hoped that government leaders could work together to achieve these goals.

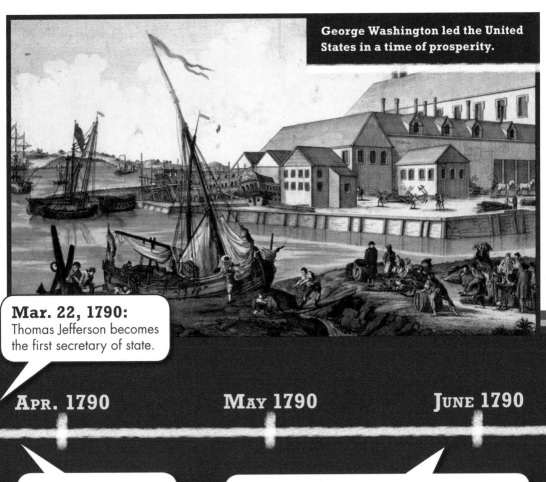

George Washington led the United States in a time of prosperity.

Mar. 22, 1790: Thomas Jefferson becomes the first secretary of state.

APR. 1790   MAY 1790   JUNE 1790

Mar. 26, 1790: A new law sets the first rules for how foreigners can become US citizens.

May 29, 1790: Rhode Island becomes the last of the original thirteen colonies to join the nation.

First Congress

Like President Washington, the US Congress was hard at work. Its first session had begun in March 1789. In all, there were twenty-six senators, two from each of the thirteen states. Each senator had been chosen by his state legislature. The House was made up of sixty-five representatives. They had been elected by the people of their state.

One of Congress's first tasks was to solve the problem of state debts. Northern states believed the federal government should pay off the states' war debts. The Funding Act of 1790 allowed the government to do just that. This made it possible for states to lower their taxes.

The first US Congress meeting took place at the Federal Hall in New York City in 1789.

July 16, 1790: The Residence Act is signed into law.

JUNE 1   JUNE 15   JULY 1   JULY 15

Summer 1790: Creek American Indians of New York and the US government sign the Treaty of New York.

July 10, 1790: Congress approves the location of the nation's future capital.

Another important decision facing Congress was the location of the nation's capital city. The country needed a permanent place for government officials to meet. In the past, they had met in Philadelphia. Then the capital moved to New York City. Congress passed the Residence Act of 1790. This law gave the president the power to select the permanent location for the government.

WASHINGTON, DC

Southern lawmakers did not want the federal capital to be in a northern city. Many had refused to support the Funding Act and the Residence Act unless President Washington chose a more centrally located capital. So Washington agreed to create a new capital closer to the South. Virginia and Maryland gave the government some of their land for this purpose. This swampy area along the Potomac River became home to a new capital city. The capital was eventually named after Washington.

Aug. 2, 1790: The first US census counts a population of 3,929,214 people.

Aug. 1   **Aug. 15**   **Sept. 1**   **Sept. 15**

Aug. 4, 1790: The Funding Act of 1790 is signed into law.

Aug. 1790: The compromises that led to the Residence and Funding Acts become known as the Compromise of 1790.

Bill of Rights and the First Bank

Congress also took up the issue of the Bill of Rights in its first session. These amendments needed the approval of three-fourths of the states. That meant the Bill of Rights would need the support of ten states.

In December 1791, Virginia became the tenth state to approve the Bill of Rights. These ten amendments then became an important part of the Constitution. The First Amendment protects Americans' freedom of speech. It also allows people to practice freedom of conscience. The Second Amendment

The Bill of Rights was created in 1789. It contains the first ten amendments to the US Constitution.

Congress of the United States,

Feb. 25, 1791: The First Bank of the United States is established.

Aug. 2, 1791: The Supreme Court hears one of its first cases.

Dec. 15, 1791: Virginia is the tenth state to ratify the Bill of Rights.

FEB. 1791   MAR.   AUG.   SEPT.   DEC.

Mar. 4, 1791: Vermont becomes the fourteenth state in the nation.

Sept. 9, 1791: The nation's capital is named after George Washington.

protects Americans' right to keep and use guns and other weapons. Other amendments establish the right to a jury in criminal cases and the right to a fair trial.

Congress also helped to establish the nation's first central bank. Secretary of the Treasury Alexander Hamilton proposed the idea. He argued that a central bank could help manage the nation's debts. It also would allow the United States to borrow money more easily in times of need. And it could help create a national mint. This mint would produce a single national currency.

Many lawmakers worried that a central bank would take power away from local banks. Still, Congress agreed to the idea. But it only gave the First Bank permission to exist for a limited time. The First Bank shut down after twenty years.

This early US coin features Lady Liberty, a symbol of democracy in the United States.

June 1, 1792: Kentucky becomes the fifteenth state in the nation.

MAR. 1792   APR.   MAY   JUNE   DEC.

Mar. 1, 1792: The adoption of the Bill of Rights is officially announced.

Dec. 5, 1792: George Washington wins the second presidential election.

Conclusion

Our nation's early leaders drafted the US Constitution more than two hundred years ago. Yet it still guides the United States. It allows the nation to create, enforce, and ensure fair laws. It has also served as a model for other emerging nations.

Americans may sometimes disagree about the meaning of parts of the US Constitution. But this document continues to reflect the careful thinking of the Founding Fathers. They did not simply imagine a government that would solve the problems of their day. They considered how the United States might grow over time.

The most important addition to the US Constitution was the Bill of Rights. It opened the

The US Constitution is a historical document that remains the foundation of our nation.

We the People

Article 1

1804: The Twelfth Amendment states that the president and the vice president should be elected together.

1913: The Seventeenth Amendment allows voters to elect their US senators.

| 1800 | 1825 | 1850 | 1875 | 1900 |

1865: The Thirteenth Amendment outlaws slavery in the nation.

1913: The Federal Reserve Act established the nation's modern central banking system.

door to future amendments to the Constitution. Many of those amendments protect the rights of the American people. Some of those people are African Americans, women, and others overlooked by the Constitution's framers.

These changes help the US Constitution remain meaningful in modern times. They help the country continue to adapt and grow. The leaders who created our nation could not have guessed what it would look like centuries later. But thanks to their efforts during the early years of the republic, their ideas live on.

The right to vote is one of many democratic principles established by the US Constitution.

1920: The Nineteenth Amendment gives women the right to vote.

1971: The Twenty-Sixth Amendment sets the voting age at eighteen.

1925   1950   1975   2000

1951: The Twenty-Second Amendment states that a US president can serve no more than two terms.

2004: The US Congress establishes Constitution Day to mark the anniversary of the US Constitution. It is observed every year on September 17.

Writing Activity

Listed below are the original ten amendments that made up the Bill of Rights. These are probably some of the most talked about amendments, especially the first two. The Supreme Court often hears cases regarding the First Amendment, and Congress continues to argue over the meaning behind the Second Amendment.

FIRST—Freedom of religion and freedom of speech

SECOND—The right to bear arms

THIRD—The right to choose not to house soldiers in your home, except in wartime

FOURTH—Protection from unnecessary searches of property

FIFTH—Protection from unfair treatment if accused of committing a crime

SIXTH and SEVENTH—The right to a speedy trial and trial by jury

EIGHTH—Protection from extreme punishment for crimes committed

NINTH—Protection of other rights not listed in the Bill of Rights

TENTH—Protection of states' rights under the Constitution

Imagine you were a member of Congress debating the amendments that needed to be included in the Bill of Rights. What amendments would you feel were missing from the US Constitution? Or are there any that you feel are unnecessary?

Write down the amendments you would like to have had added to the US Constitution. Then explain how your amendment would have affected people's lives. How would your proposed amendments affect people today?

Glossary

amendment: a change or addition to an official US document

constitution: a document that contains the principles and laws that govern a country

currency: the form money takes, such as paper bills and coins

debt: borrowed money that is owed to the lender

delegate: someone who represents a group at a meeting

federal: related to a nation's central government

legislature: an organized group of people who have the authority to make laws

populous: containing many people

ratify: to approve something, such as an amendment

republic: a country that is governed by elected leaders instead of by a king or a queen

tax: money an individual pays to a local, state, or national government

treaty: a written agreement between nations

unanimous: agreed to by everyone

LERNER
SOURCE

Expand learning beyond the printed book. Download free, complementary educational resources for this book from our website, www.lerneresource.com.

Further Information

The American Revolution
http://www.theamericanrevolution.org
This site is full of information about the Revolutionary War.

The Charters of Freedom
http://www.archives.gov/exhibits/charters
Visit this site to learn more about some of the most influential documents in US history.

Morey, Allan. *A Timeline History of the Declaration of Independence*. Minneapolis: Lerner Publications, 2015. Learn about the important events that led to the Declaration of Independence.

Our Documents
http://www.ourdocuments.gov/index.php?flash=true&
Visit this site to see copies of famous US documents, from the Articles of Confederation to the Declaration of Independence.

Ransom, Candice. *Who Wrote the US Constitution? And Other Questions about the Constitutional Convention of 1787*. Minneapolis: Lerner Publications, 2011. Explore this book to learn more details about the Constitutional Convention.

Schmidt, Maegan. *The US Constitution and Bill of Rights*. Minneapolis: Abdo, 2013. Find out more about events that took place during the Constitutional Convention.

Sharp, Constance. *America Is Born (1770–1800)*. Broomall, PA: Mason Crest Publishers, 2012. This book presents the early history behind the forming of the United States of America.

US Department of State, Office of the Historian—Milestones: 1784–1800
http://history.state.gov/milestones/1784-1800
This site covers important events during the early years of the United States.

Index

Photo Acknowledgements

The images in this book are used with the permission of: Architect of the Capitol, pp. 4–5, 16; National Archives arc 301687, p. 7; © MPI/Archive Photos/Getty Images, p. 8; © US Army Center of Military History, p. 10; Smallbones/Wikimedia Commons (CC0 1.0), p. 11; The Granger Collection, New York, p. 12; Courtesy Everett Collection, p. 13; Wikimedia Commons, pp. 14, 29 (left); © North Wind Picture Archives/Alamy, p.15; © DeAgostini/SuperStock, p. 19; © Stock Montage/Archive Photos/Getty Images, pp. 20, 22, 34–35; © SuperStock/Everett Collection, pp. 20–21; © Universal Images Group/Getty Images, p. 23; © Hulton Archive/Getty Images, p. 24; Library of Congress LC-DIG-pga-02419, p. 25; © Private Collection/The Bridgeman Art Library, p. 27; Library of Congress LC-DIG-ppmsca-19166, p. 28 (left); Library of Congress LC-USZ62-70508, p. 29 (right); © Collection of the New-York Historical Society, USA/The Bridgeman Art Library, p. 30; Gilbert Stuart, John Adams, Ailsa Mellon Bruce Fund, image courtesy of the Board of Trustees, National Gallery of Art, Washington, DC, p. 31; © Members of George Washington's First Government Cabinet, February 1789, by Alonzo Chappel, Engraving, 1879/J. T. Vintage/The Bridgeman Art Library, p. 32; Gilbert Stuart, George Washington, gift of Thomas Jefferson Coolidge IV in memory of his great-grandfather, Thomas Jefferson Coolidge, his grandfather, Thomas Jefferson Coolidge II, and his father, Thomas Jefferson Coolidge III, image courtesy of the Board of Trustees, National Gallery of Art, Washington, DC, p. 33; © Kean Collection/Archive Photos/Getty Images, p. 34; Library of Congress LC-USZC4-41172, p. 37; Library of Congress LC-DIG-ppmsca-15703, p. 38; photograph by Robin Miller, courtesy Independence National Historic Park, p. 39; National Archives 1408042, p. 40; AP Photo/PR NEWSWIRE, p. 41; National Archives 1667751, p. 42; © Americanspirit/Dreamstime.com, p. 43.

Front Cover: PHGCOM/Wikimedia Commons.

Main text font set in Caecilia Com 55 Rom 11/16.
Typeface provided by Linotype AG.